Note from the Transition:

As a closing act for the Transition, Senior Advisor Valerie Jarrett requested that the Office of Public Liaison create a process by which Americans outside of Washington could come together to present ideas directly to the President – a "Citizen's Briefing Book."

The idea was to use the Transition website, change.gov, to create a grassroots version of the research binders that presidents receive every day. But instead of advice from top government officials, the Citizen's Briefing Book is composed of ideas submitted by ordinary people and reflecting the enthusiastic engagement from the public we saw throughout the course of Change.gov.

125,000 users submitted over 44,000 ideas and cast over 1.4 million votes, with the most popular ideas accumulating tens of thousands of votes each. This book contains some of the top ideas, broken into groups by issue area. You can tell how popular each idea was by looking at the number next to it – it represents how many people voted for the idea, with 10 points awarded for each positive vote. In addition, you will find a "word cloud" for each category of ideas representing the frequency with which various words and concepts appeared through the entire process.

Out of the tens of thousands of submissions, these ideas found the most support; here they are, unvarnished and unedited.

Contents

Economy

Word Cloud

Revoke the George W. Bush tax cuts for the top 1%, 57080 points

> The notion that giving the owners of the companies more money so that it will eventually trickle down to the common people is absurd. People WITH money HAVE money because they know how to KEEP money.
>
> -- *http://warismyconcern.wordpress.com*

Let's make reduced-scale farming profitable! Less dependence on imported foods! 42070 points

> Large, industrial, corporate farms have driven the smaller, local-based food production farms into non-existance. It is the combination of the productions from these larger farms and food imported from other countries that feeds this nation. We need to reduce our dependence on these other nations. It will help our own economy, reduce fuel use and emmisions, and bring back a natural part of any healthy society -- a succesfull agricultural system!
>
> A trend has been growing over the last few years promoting and advocating the purchasing of products from these local farms, but more needs to be done to complete the vision of an agriculturally self-sufficient nation. Only through the efforts of local growers, consumers, purchasers, stores, and governments will this vision be achieved... the large corporations and farm systems are simply too big for the 'little man' to work with. There is still room for these large farms in the

bigger picture, but we MUST HAVE access to local produce, meats, dairy products, and materials to fill the needs of a nation that has a large population and a large need for healty, fresh food.
-- aplkorex

Reform the IRS and Stop the Tax Loopholes, **32840 points**

Stop taxing the poor and the middle class and stop the rich from avoiding taxes. In his article entitled : "Fiscal Therapy" found at http://www.motherjones.com/news/feature/2009/01/fiscal-therapy.html the author talks about some of the loop holes in our tax system and that the IRS needs to be brought to the 21st century.

The author David Cay Johnston, in his article entitled: Fiscal Therapy says: "End Legal Tax Cheating. The marginal tax rate for cops and teachers is more than 40 percent—25 percent for income taxes and another 15 percent for Social Security and Medicare taxes. The marginal rate for some hedge fund managers, five of whom earned more than $1 billion in 2007, has been zero. That's because many of these speculators have been able to avoid taxes by operating through offshore partnerships under rules that let them defer income taxes. Executives, entertainers, and athletes also have been able to amass vast untaxed fortunes: For example, Roberto C. Goizueta, the ceo of Coca-Cola in the '80s and '90s, built a nest egg of more than $1 billion, but was able to defer taxes on most of it until he died."

Please read the rest of the article. I am sure all his points can be verified with a little research.

Thank you
-- gems

Encourage Trade Schools, **32150 points**

Learning a trade, or two, should be encouraged as an alternative to college.
There are lots of things we spend an exorbiant amount of money on, other than cars, that could benefit good repair technicians. We have this idea that if something is on the blitz we should immediately throw it away and buy another because we know the company will not send anyone out to fix it.

Along with the potential to stay employed in a bad economy, it would at the very least reduce our waste output. I believe it is also one of the reasons why so many of our jobs have been outsourced.
-- Tynil

More Stimulus Focus on Green Jobs, **30470 points**

Green jobs was the promise and green jobs rather than old style support jobs for the oil-based system of highways etc. should be the funding focus of economic stimulus right now.
-- Dr. J

Education

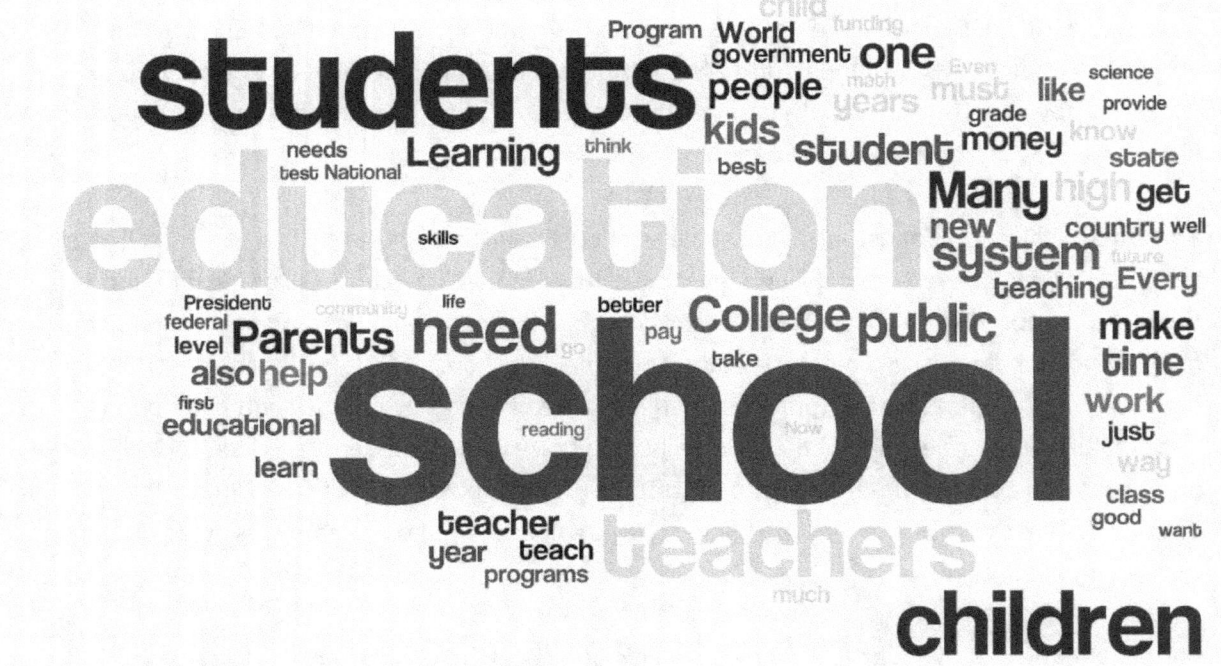

An end to the government sponsored abstinence education to be replaced by an introduction of age appropriate sex education, 65350 points

> 1-4 teenagers have a sexually transmitted disease. AIDS still exists. The longer we keep our children in the dark about their bodies, the longer these facts will continue to be true. The longer we endanger the very children we seek to protect. Sex WILL happen. As adults our own histories have proven that. It is wrong to expect more from our children than we could from ourselves. We can, however, help them to understand the consequences and beauties of the decisions they choose to make. I do NOT imply that sex education will solve the world's problems. I DO mean to imply that when teenagers understand the gravity of what they possess and all of its dangers they will make decisions that are more adult in nature. Sex is an adult decision. I agree. I also agree that the decision to not have sex is also an adult decision. Informing our youth is part of helping them grow. We cripple them with fear tactics, when we could instead empower them to live safe, responsible lives.
>
> *-- http://warismyconcern.wordpress.com*

Healthy Kids Learn Better, **15060 points**

> Connect local farms with nearby schools, institutions and shelters to ensure that we are encouraging and supporting farmers so they may produce healthy local commodities to promote a healthy local community. I am mostly concerned about school caferterias. We should evalu-

ate and enhance the USDA programs that regulates vendors that provide food for schools and other institutues. Due to tight budgets (or lack of nutritional training) school caferterias are providing low quality food to our children. A chicken nugget that is filled with preservatives and breading shouldn't be considered as a protein when ensuring that our children are eating a nutritionally balanced meal. Schools are serving sugary, fattening foods to our children filled with MSG and other harmful additives. They are teaching our children that this is the way to eat. As a concerned parent I have questioned them and they say that they are limited by their budget and approved vendors. Some of the children can only count on the food that they get from and eat at school. Shouldn't we demand that children get a high quality protein breakfast every morning and a well balanced high quality lunch and afternoon snack along with daily physical exercise to ensure our children can meet their highest potential.

I do not have all the solutions but I do think this should be part of the discussion when it comes to education, health care, nutrition and the environment.

-- Healthy Kids Advocate

Focus on the Art and Creativity, **12970 points**

It is always the arts that are first to be cut back in our schools and communities, yet the arts are at the very center of creativity. This is where creative skills are born, not just for artists and musicians, but for scientists, engineers, researchers, innovators, and all thinking peoples. Now, if ever, is the time when we need creative thought and creative action to find the means and the human energy and spirit to find our way out of the problems that face us.

-- Maples

Libraries of all types need our support, **10810 points**

"The library connects us with the insight and knowledge, painfully extracted from Nature, of the greatest minds that ever were, with the best teachers, drawn from the entire planet and from all our history, to instruct us without tiring, and to inspire us to make our own contribution to the collective knowledge of the human species. I think the health of our civilization, the depth of our awareness about the underpinnings of our culture and our concern for the future can all be tested by how well we support our libraries." ~Carl Sagan, Cosmos

Carl said it best. Please continue and expand upon the support provided to libraries of all types.

-- NJ Busch

Lost SCIENTISTS and ENGINEERS, **10480 points**

Our great NASA's Scientists & Engineers "IN TOTAL" are less than China graduates in a single year!!! We are not the innovators anymore, and we need the Safety, Security, and prosperity it brings to our country. For a committed period of time, Scientist & Engineer degree programs should be FREE to any American with the apptitude. We need this as a country to be the greatest again.

--Brain Labor

Energy & Environment

Word Cloud

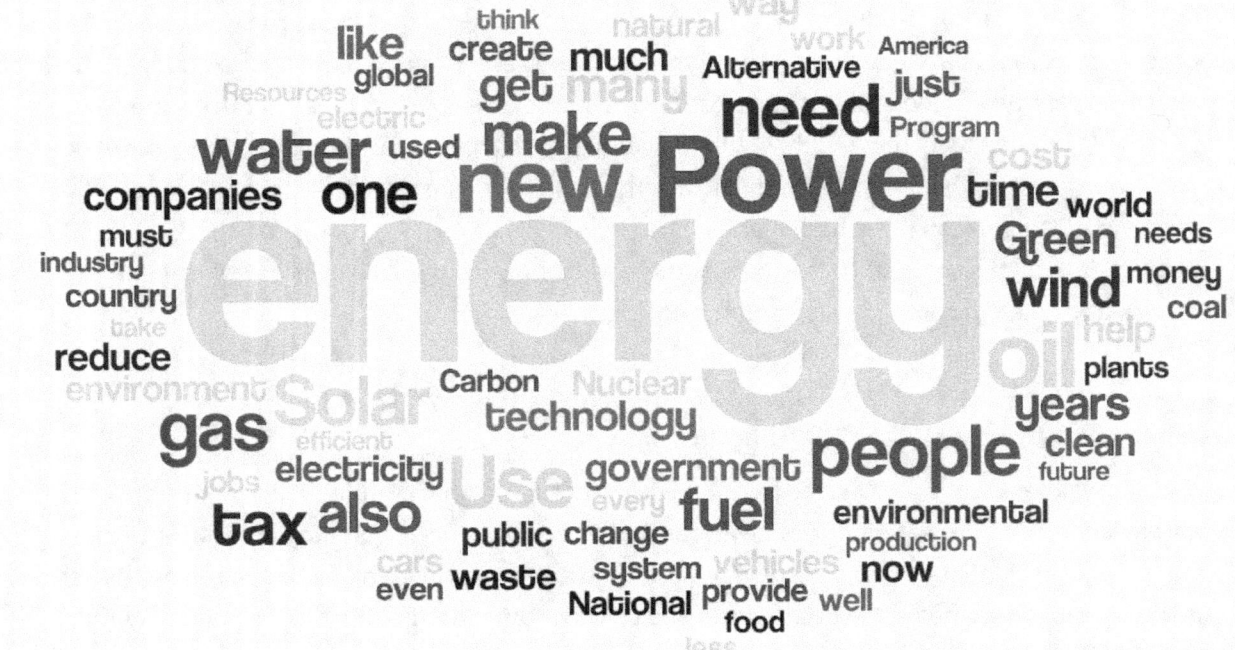

Commit to becoming the "Greenest" country in the world, 70470 points

If America committed itself to this creed it would solve many problems at once. By creating the economic incentives and legislative benchmarks, going green will:

- Completely revamp American industries and help them compete in global markets.

- Save America's auto industries by creating a change or fail incentives.

- Put millions of people back to work.

- Rebuild our infrastructure in ways that provide everyone with clean safe transportation.

- Eliminate America's need for foreign oil (by 2020 not 2050) making America safer.

- Renew the American Dream and restore America's leadership and respect in the world.

Thank you.

-- Rob Beeson

Bullet Trains & Light Rail, 65100 points

Train transportation funding should be increased at the federal level. I think that the one issue keeping many people from using trains to travel to and from other cities is that they are too slow. What we really need are bullet trains between cities, like the ones that are prevalent in Japan.

To increase the number of individuals using trains, the trains have to be much faster, and have to arrive at terminals at a greater frequency

Additionally, more funding should be removed from road construction and moved to funding light rail initiatives in major U.S. cities.
-- J.M. Lee

Increase MPG requirements now! **46120 points**

After spending tens of billions of dollars in taxpayer money to bail out poorly run domestic auto makers, maybe we should make it a requirement that they focus any/all taxpayer money into improving their product to relieve America dependency on foreign oil.

If we want US automakers to be successful again, it's time to stop making Escalades and start selling affordable products that will benefit the micro and macro Economies in the US, not to mention the Environment.
-- M. Johnson

Implement a National High-Speed Rail Program, **38720 points**

A true high-speed rail system, with electric trains running at 150-200 miles per hour in the country's most heavily travelled corridors, would do a lot to improve the mobility of America's citizens. Building such a network, much like constructing the Interstate Highway System, would employ thousands of people, providing a beneficial economic stimulus. It would provide individuals with an environmentally-friendly, fast, and comfortable alternative to automobiles and airplanes. And it would help restore the health of many of our nation's inner cities.
-- Yonah Freemark

Re-install the White House solar panels, **28910 points**

Make the White house an example of "Green" living. You may not have agreed with the Presidency of Jimmy Carter but I think we can all agree that he was right when it came to our dependency on oil. Take this action further by making all government and state buildings "green." If the government buildings are "green" and the cars that they drive are "green" then the evolution of "green living" is fostered by example.
-- http://warismyconcern.wordpress.com

Foreign Policy

Word Cloud

The permanent closure of all Torture facilities. (Facilities such as: Guantanamo, and Abu Ghraib), 61250 points

Let us again be human rights advocates. Torture is a popular debate in the current American discourse. The reaction of the US to photographs of our smiling soldiers at Abu Grahib made clear that America is no longer the defender of human rights. The reality of war is that horrible things happen. We know this. We are not alone in this knowledge. Torture is not new. The world knows this. What has changed is our public stance on human rights violations such as torture. As a country, we now condone torture openly, which is far different than merely knowing that it happens in war. Most parents know that their children drink from time to time but they do not condone it. Condoning torture is the beginning of devolution.

-- http://warismyconcern.wordpress.com

Re-evaluate aid to Israel, 37240 points

Re-evaluate aid to Israel

Reevaluate whether the level of and the basis for the aid we provide Israel is appropriate given our tough economic circumstance. Presently I fail to see the benefits to our country that would justify the extraordinarily high per-capita level of aid.

-- Citizen Cyr

Time for CHANGE in Cuba, **18020 points**

Dear President Obama,

I recently returned from taking my daughter on a OFAC approved family visit to Cuba. Please show my eight year old daughter that we supported the right presidential candidate by allowing her to visit her 85 year old great grandmother, 91 year old great uncle and 94 year old great aunt when whenever we choose,

Thank you
-- ChiChi

Close School of the Americas (WHINSEC), **17610 points**

Dear President Obama, The School of the Americas (renamed the Western Hemisphere Institute for Security Cooperation) is part of the conventional thinking that military repression is a solution to social and political problems. The existence of the SOA/ WHINSEC is part of a larger failure in U.S. foreign policy towards Latin America. It is a symbol of oppression and U.S. domination for most Latin Americans and should be shut down without delay. I am urging you to issue an executive order to close down the School of the Americas (SOA/WHINSEC)
-- pagz4u

Engage strongly for Israeli-Palestinian peace, **13990 points**

The crisis in Gaza is further evidence of the tragic consequences of American disengagement from Middle East diplomacy. President-elect Obama must make strong American leadership to bring about a two-state solution to the Israeli-Palestinian conflict an urgent priority of his foreign policy agenda, starting on day one.

Time is about to run out on the two-state solution. The U.S. can no longer simply facilitate discussions, we need to actively put the solutions on the table and bring the parties to agreement. Ending this conflict is an essential American interest, vital to our efforts to address other threats in the region and to restoring our reputation around the world.
-- Isaac @ J Street

Health Care

Word Cloud

Stop using federal resources to undermine states' medicinal marijuana laws, 66170 points

> Our federal government's Drug Enforcement Administration continues to raid marijuana (cannabis) dispensaries and compassionate use clubs in locations where local and state law allows them to operate. Medicinal marijuana is one of the most widely-supported issues in drug policy reform. Our federal government is wasting scarce resources -- and hurting sick people -- by arresting patients and their caregivers; it should stop doing so.
>
> *-- Phil Mocek*

Get the Insurance Companies out the Health Care, 55080 points

> The reason that our country pays more for health care than anywhere else in the world and still has poor health outcomes is that the system is run by profit-seeking insurance companies. Health insurance should not be a for-profit field.
>
> *-- T. Desmond*

Allow the terminally ill the honor of passing as they choose, 40850 points

> Families huddle together across the country struggling with life and death decisions for their loved ones. The opinions of Congress have no business in these painfully personal decisions. Teri Schivo was a perfect example of Congress "acting on behalf of the public" when they should have stayed home. If a dying family member makes a psychologically sound decision to end their

pain then they should be allowed to pass as they please. If doctors have done all that they can do for an unresponsive patient and enough time has passed for a miracle to have happened then it is understandable and humane that a family might choose to shut down the machines that push breath through lungs that no longer live. Know your place as members of Congress; we know our place as citizens.

-- http://warismyconcern.wordpress.com

Health Freedom IS Our First Freedom, **30430 points**

Health Freedom - Our First Freedom!

Health Freedom means the right to control what happens to your body, choosing your own health path, making our own health choices as you see fit.

Please vote for health freedom so we can have:
Access to high potency nutrients and supplements
Protection from Codex
Absolute medical privacy
Meaningful organic standards
Access to raw milk, bitter almonds and other health aides
Irradiation-free foods

Freedom from:
- Unlabelled GMO foods
- Coercedor mandatory vaccinations and other medical treatments including psychiatric or other drugging
- Involuntary experimentation on foster children, prisoners and civilian populations
- Chemtrail spraying
- Coerced/mandatory surgical or other procedures such as infant circumcision or electroshock for children or adults
- Human or animal chipping
- Loss of our children because we choose not to vaccinate or drug them

Freedom to:
- Choose health practitioners who offer the treatments we want
- Farm and process food
- Provide information about the relationship between health and foods/nutrients
- Drink municipal water free of fluoride and other toxins
- Receive insurance coverage for natural medicine
- Divest the FDA of all food regulation.
- Sue drug and vaccine manufacturers for damages caused by their products
- Use natural methods to treat, prevent, mitigate or cure diseases as we choose

- Protect our children as we, not authorities, see fit
- Give birth under the circumstances we see fit

-- JJ Monte

Increased Funding for Childhood Cancer, **16500 points**

Dear President Obama:

Childhood cancer is the number one killer disease of our children today: More than from asthma, diabetes, cystic fibrosis, congenital anomalies, and pediatric AIDS combined. Our children, your children, have a 1 in 300 chance of being diagnosed with cancer before age 20. Each school day, 46 more children are diagnosed. Survival rates, while improving, have leveled at around 75%; and each day 7 children die from cancer. In addition, each day, nearly 40,000 children are in treatment.

Treatments for childhood cancer have not changed for 20 years, with "down-sized" adult treatments being the primary means. These treatments leave 60% of the SURVIVORS with long-term health issues ranging from infertility to developmental problems to major organ damage to higher risk for secondary cancers.

Yet funding for our children's number one killer is woefully inadequate. Our generation has mobilized against breast, color and prostate cancer, yet we have grossly failed our children in funding improvements in their care. Funding for research into prostate cancer is over $2000 for each year of potential life lost. Similarly, colon cancer and breast cancer receive approximately $350 and $150 respectively for each year of potential life lost. Childhood cancer receives about $23 for each year of potential life lost. We are ashamed.

I did not know this until Father's Day 2007 when my 14 year old son AJ was diagnosed with cancer. He was a happy, healthy, athletic young man that was a joy to be around. He supported you. Unfortunately, in December 2008, I was forced to answer a question I hope no other Dad ever hears: "Dad, what is hospice?" AJ left us on January 5, 2008.

But as promised, we fight back. I, along with an incredible young woman who has survived childhood cancer, have founded People Against Childhood Cancer, or PAC2 (www.curechildhood-cancer.ning.com). In four months we are over 3,000 strong and will never stop on behalf of the children we love. We seek ways to increase funding for this horrible elephant in the room that America refuses to acknowledge.

The NCI and the American Cancer Society direct less than 3% of all funding to childhood cancer. Last year, a huge victory for the childhood cancer community was the Carolyn Price Conquer Childhood Cancer Act, allocating $25 million for the next five years for childhood cancer research. In today's world of billions and trillions, much of it going to those that barely deserve it,

I again have to be ashamed.

We are not protecting the youngest and most innocent of our society to the best of our abilities. You have the power to directly fund more research in your budget. Please consider including a major line item in your budget to fund research to save our children. We are sure Malia Ann and Natasha would approve.

Sincerely,

Bob Piniewski and Lori Keith
Founders – People Against Childhood Cancer
-- AJs Dad

Homeland Security

Word Cloud

No More Wars On Abstract Concepts, **38250 points**

We've had the "War on Terror" and the "War on Drugs". Neither of these had any clear goals or strategy, but were instead a catch-all banner for spending money without having to show results. The results have been devastating, and have only increased the problems they were supposed to solve.

If the president is to use the word "war" when asking the nation for its dollars and other sacrifices, that "war" should be against a specific target -- geographical or political -- with measurable criteria of achievement, and an exit strategy if it doesn't achieve what was expected. Congress should have to approve any substantial changes or extensions to that plan.

No future president should have the kind of carte blanche which was granted to Bush, and which resulted in the horrors of Iraq, Abu Ghraib, and Guantanamo.
-- *Woozle*

Enact legislation that protects "whistle blowers" **36390 points**

Across the nation secrets are being guarded by everyday citizens. People employed to monitor our drinking water, research our environment, mediate our commerce, gather foreign intelligence, guard our ports, review our taxes, instruct our children, welcome our veterans, invent our cures...so on and so forth. They are the closest monitors we have to regulate genuine safety in society. When they speak out, we should listen. When their claims are proven to be true, we should thank them by ensuring protection from the many forms of retaliation that inevitably manifest when defending Americans from negative motivations. These "whistleblowers" speak out because they see harm being done, not because they look forward to risking the future of their families. Unfortunately, for these brave people, retaliation outweighs thanks received. For those who speak out in defense of our nation, citizens and employees must have the freedom to protect society.

-- http://warismyconcern.wordpress.com

Eliminate Don't Ask, Don't Tell so we don't lose any more soldiers, **35840 points**

During a time of war, the military has discharged soldiers fluent in Arabic and Farsi because of their sexuality. Who cares who they fall in love with? Our country needs to be protected.

As many qualified officers have already said: Don't Ask, Don't Tell is a failed policy and should be immediately suspended.

-- Joshua Coker

A New Decentralized Energy Grid, **14920 points**

We desperately need a new Decentralized Energy Grid (DEG). If implemented intelligently, (Thomas Friedman's Hot, Flat and Crowded) this grid would:

- Make America safer from Terrorism and Cyber-Terrorism.

- It would put millions of Americans back to work.

- It would encourage local green energy generation that would share the profits between the utilities and the consumers.

Thank you,
Rob
-- Rob Beeson

Find a Balance Between US Security and Civil Liberties, **15660 points**

With the reversal of many civil liberties by the Bush administration in the past eight years in the name of Terrorism, we need to find a balance between protecting our country without giving up our cherished rights as American Citizens. I am hoping a balance can be met without giving agencies carte blanche and no oversight.

-- Admiralu

Service

Word Cloud

National Service Corps, **9350 points**

We need to expand, or perhaps create anew, Americorps. There needs to be an organized fashion in which the youth of this country are required to serve it. Israeli citizens are required to serve in the army of their country, and that makes sense for such a small population in their somewhat precarious position.

We don't need everyone to serve in the military. But the present feeling in this country that we're "entitled" to the best handed to us on a silver platter has GOT TO GO. If every high school graduate were required to do a year or two of public service - helping in nursing homes or visiting shut ins, delivering Meals on Wheels, working in the VA hospitals, working on public works projects, whatever - it would accomplish many thing, but two most important.
-- Kate E.

Create an online E-Library, **8100 points**

Start a program scanning the library of congress into an online library where it can be accessed for free. It would make it so much easier and cheaper for public/ school libraries to offer the people they serve quality access to knowledge. Going hand in hand with the plan already in place to drastically expand broadband lines and invest in 21st century schools, this would do much to improve American education while making it more cost effective. It would also save money and the enviornement by reducing the amount of paper purchased by the government when stocking multiple libraries with the same books.

-- Kevin J. Kauth

Expand Small Business Innovation Programs, **6550 points**

The Small Business Innovation Research (SBIR) program has been providing near-term growth with long-term benefits for many years now. It is an established yet dynamic program created and administered by the federal government. http://www.sba.gov/aboutsba/sbaprograms/sbir/index.html

Because the program administration and guidelines are already in place, an expansion of the program could be accomplished almost overnight, perhaps by merely generalizing a previous Executive Order (for example, 13329).

-- Next Generation

National Service program, **6250 points**

Develop programs which provide minimal salary (perhaps plus room and board) for high school graduates (perhaps college) to serve in Health Care, education. National Parks, construction of low cost housing, weatherization of public buildings. An apprenticeshp program to give young graduates enough experience to f nd out if this is a life career while still making a "basic trainee" level salary. Perhaps this program could become mandatory as an alternatvie to military service.

-- punahou

National Service for College Students, **4850 points**

College students over the summertime are looking for ways to connect themselves to each other and their country.

Set up a National Program that allows college students to travel and volunteer time in communities all over our country. Create a resource that allows locals to "host a student" for the summertime who is volunteering in the community (much like foreign exchange).

Set it up at the National level to allow students to find opportunities that fit interests and skillsets that they have.

Setup geographically appropriate training hubs for people to learn special skills (like the army) to bring back to their own communities. Foster a sense of generational pride where older kids pass the torch to younger kids, and where people can meet and form friendships through common purpose.

Also see my other related idea, "Facebook for National Service"

-- kong

Technology

Word Cloud

Boost America's Economy with Legal Online Poker, 46890 points

> Let online poker players in the United States play legally and without fear of prosecution. Reform the Unlawful Internet Gambling Enforcement Act to exempt poker, a game of skill, from the law. Boost the economy by letting American companies and Ameican players make money and pay taxes instead of sending online poker businesses offshore. Protect online poker players by regulating the industry to ensure that no one is ever cheated.
>
> *-- AAHue*

Restore Net Neutrality Protections to the Internet, 46220 points

> During the campaign, Barack Obama pledged to "take a backseat to no one in my commitment to Net Neutrality" and to "protect the Internet's traditional openness to innovation and creativity and ensure that it remains a platform for free speech and innovation that will revitalize our democracy." The administration can show it's commitment by working with the new Congress and FCC to pass laws that make Net Neutrality the cornerstone to protecting innovation, free speech and choice on the Internet.
>
> *-- TimKarr*

Vote and debate all bills online and show what industries contribute the most to each Representatives campaign, 40080 points

Vote and debate all bills online and show what industries contribute the most to each Representatives campaign while they are voting. Let's show the American people who really run the country!

-- JimBO

Each of the 50 State Governors should create a version of this site to gather ideas from their constituents, 25730 points

Each of the 50 states should create a version of this site so that citizens can share ideas directly with their state and local government officials.

-- Daniel

National WiFi, 23540 points

Internet access in the new emerging world and culture needs to be a right and not a privilage. Those who cannot afford broadband access will be left behind dispreportionately. Broadband Internet Access needs to be avalible to all Americans and most especially to those who can't afford it. Let's make this a priority.

Further National WiFi access will broaden new business opportunities in a new emerging economy. Americans could have cell phones that have no service fees, internet access at any location and the ability to be in contact with anyone or anything instantly. The possibilites are endless.

-- Jesse E

Veterans

Word Cloud

Signing bonuses for enlistment should not be revoked due to injuries beyond the control of the soldiers who risk their lives to save ours, 14530 points

A rash of wounded soldiers are coming home with life-changing injuries only to find that the government now expects them to re-pay their signing bonus because they were injured too early in their service. How is this supporting our troops?

-- *http://warismyconcern.wordpress.com*

Our military have been subjected to unacceptable tour extensions, 7460 points

The stop-loss clauses in the military contracts have been abused and this should be addressed sooner rather than later. Suicide amongst veterans returning from Iraq has reached levels of which this country has never seen. Yet we continue to "support our troops" by expecting them to serve tour after tour with no end in sight. Human being are not built like that. Wars are not won like that.

-- *http://warismyconcern.wordpress.com*

Upon exiting the military every soldier must be given formal notice in writing, using clearly spoken language, a detailed synopsis of their medical benefits, 6320 points

In addition each veteran should be assigned a case worker, with a manageable work-load, that can easily navigate the bureaucracy required to obtain those benefits. We have too many sick veterans. We have too many homeless veterans. They have waited too long for the respect that they deserve. Don't let them become just another loophole exploited by the greed of the power-ful few.

-- *http://warismyconcern.wordpress.com*

Ensure that veterans suffering from exposure to Agent Orange are fully covered by their VA ben-efits, **5710 points**

This must include veteran's deployed sold ers in bordering countries to where Agent Orange was used, all veterans deployed in countries that Agent Orange was transported through, and any veterans affected by military tests of Agert Orange. As a nation, we continue to leave behind those who have given us their all and that is reprehensible.

-- *http://warismyconcern.wordpress.com*

VA Hospital Reform now, **3560 points**

As a country we were shocked to learn of the conditions that existed at the Walter Reed VA facil-ity. It turns out that these conditions are not shocking at all. Veterans who depend on these ser-vices tell story upon story of the inadequate care, un-kept hosp tals, struggles to qualify for care, and endless paper work that impedes care. We owe them more.As a country we were shocked to learn of the conditions that existed at the Walter Reed VA facility. It turns out that these condi-tions are not shocking at all. Veterans who depend on these services tell story upon story of the inadequate care, un-kept hospitals, struggles to qualify for care, and endless paper work that impedes care. We owe them more.

-- *http://warismyconcern.wordpress.com*

Additional Issues

Word Cloud

Ending Marijuana Prohibition, **92970 points**

I suggest that we step back and take a non-biased "Science Based" approach to decide what should be done about the "Utter Failure" that we call the War on (some) Drugs.

The fact is that Marijuana is much less harmful to our bodies than other Legal Drugs such as Tobacco and Alcohol. And for the Government to recognize Marijuana as having Medicinal Properties AND as a Schedule I drug (Has NO medicinal Properties) is an obvious flaw in the system. We must stop imprisoning responsible adult citizens choosing to use a drug that has been mislabeled for over 70 years.

-- *Matt*

Revoke the Tax Exempt Status of the Church of Scientology, **52470 points**

The Church of Scientology was founded in the early 1950s, and quickly gained and lost its tax exempt status as a religion. The IRS ruled that the system of "fixed donations" and the services offered to the public constituted a for-profit venture, and was therefore taxable. This judgement stood the test of the courts, and was only overturned after the Church of Scientology filed more than 2,000 law suits against the IRS and individuals within the organization. Scientology leader David Miscavige met with IRS officials to negotiate their new tax deal, one which is clearly superior to those of all other religious organizations in the United States.

In the recent Skylar case, it was ruled that similar tax exemptions for religious schooling should not be allowed for the Jewish couple. Based on this ruling, it is mandatory to maintain the Establishment Clause of the Constitution that Scientology's tax exempt status at the very least be altered so as to match those of other religions.

It is my belief, and the belief of thousands of other Americans, that the Church of Scientology is a dangerous, for-profit organization. Thousands of accusations of abuse have been leveled against the church, both domestically and internationally, and the organization has been convicted of fraud and manslaughter in some countries. Such an organization does not deserve the same tax breaks as other religions, and it certainly does not deserve better ones.

-- azure

Bring Back the Constitution! **50160 points**

1. Separation of church and state.
2. Free speech.
3. Right to be secure "in our persons and effects".
4. Rights to Life, Liberty and the pursuit of Happiness, so long as we infringe on no on else's same rights.
5. Right to bear arms.
6. Right to a speedy trial.
7. Respect for other sovereign nations.
etc.

These rights are clear and not to be violated. What have we become? What are we without these things? Why are they termed "ambiguous"? What would Jefferson think of us now?

Are we the United States of the Federal Reserve? Its lackeys, thinking we are making any difference with all this political stuff?

-- Angroid

Honesty and Transparency, **45610 points**

Whatever the issue -- economy, energy, forgein policy, health care, homeland security, or other -- it is most important that honesty and transparency guide the debate. In communicating with the American people, the President and his representatives must remain true to the principles of honesty and transparency.

-- GeneL

people talking to government, **41740 points**

One of the problems with politcs is that the people's voice isn't heard. This website is amazing! Please expand this so that people can vote on things that congress votes on. This will show congress what the constituants want. You can have the people vote on items and then show how their congress people voted on the same issue. It's been too long that a small, discorrected group of people control the lives of the US population. The American people have NOT stood up. Expand this website so that the people's voice can be heard again. Great job with change.gov. WE WANT MORE!

-- aDAM

End the "War" Against American Citizens, **40510 points**

The "War" on Drugs has been shown over and over again to be an utter failure. Over 70 years and trillions of tax dollars spent and what do we have to show for it? The highest non-violent prison population in the world and more affordable illegal drugs with higher purities and high chances for adulteration.

We need to learn from our history. If you do not learn from history you are doomed to repeat it. Which we've done time and again. Prohibition creates crime, during the prohibition of alcohol we had some of the most notorious gangsters in the U. S. smuggling alcohol and killing people. And the same holds true with the prohibtion of any drug. And yes alcohol is a drug.

And I'm not saying that change is easy, it's not, many need to be shown the error of their ways. Many don't even know the truth about most drugs, especially since our government has lied to us for years about the true dangers and benefits of drugs. Many seem to think that prescription meds are completely safe, yet they can be some of the worst for side effects.

Many of the drugs that are illegal today were used by ancient cultures for spiritual fulfillment. And a look at the history of our prohibition of drugs shows that all were made that way due to many people's racism. And the propaganda used is obviously and blatantly false. D.A.R.E. does nothing to deter children from using drugs at some point, because when you see anecdotal evidence in front of you that using those drugs doesn't turn you into the deliquent that they portray, then you've lost your ability to have people believe you. Unfortunately many do follow blindly and it's to be expected that people want to trust the government, yet the whole basis of this country is to always question your government, always be keeping them in check. Nobody is infalible.

We must learn from our mistakes and quit continuing to make the same ones. And of course it sounds horrible to say we need to legalize all of these hard drugs, but when it comes down to it, if you tax it, regulate and educate people on it, they will use it much more responsibly. And who says that adults need a babysitter to tell them how to run their lives? Yes, we see alcohol ruin lives, and smoking cigarettes definitely causes many problems. Yet people are allowed the right to choose to use those products. And some cannot handle it and they get help. They have healthcare and support groups. But for the price you pay for the repeal of prohibition, would you bring it back to wipe out alcohol again and strive for a truly "drug-free" society?

A war against your own people is wrong, and honestly should be considered tyranny. And the American people are supposed to rise up against tyranny. Yet we cannot because we also have been nearly stripped of the second amendment as well.

Don't we have much better things to spend our money on? In this time of economic crisis, shouldn't we eliminate spending where it's not needed as much? Couldn't a great tax profit be made by the U.S. on repealing prohibition? We would also free up our police forces to fight real crimes, like the murders that we have in our city every summer. Or the rapes and child abuse and molestation cases. Or the theft, robbery and burglary that we constantly see because of the horrid economy. I personally have been robbed twice and have yet to hear anything back about my stolen property. Thousands of dollars worth of audio equipment that I received through birthdays and Christmases from family. Yet they're too busy to find the people that do those things.

How bad does it sound to be the world's leading jailer when you have the world's 4th largest population? We've got more inmates that we've got room for and most are just regular people that were just trying to get by. And they chose a substance other than alcohol or tobacco. Sit down and talk to some of them, it's hard to say that they ruin your life completely when you can see people in the media touting their use and showing the money that they have been able to earn working or acting or being an artist.

Speak with the members of Law Enforcement Against Prohibition and they will give you first hand the devastation that prohibition brings. They can tell you straight from the horses mouth what they've seen and what they would do to end it. And these are the people that are here to serve and protect us. They are the people you should give your utmost respect to because they put their lives on the line every day to help make this world a better place and I'm sure they'd like to be putting many more violent people away as well.

If you want to be the President of the People Mr. Obama sir, you should listen to all of the people. Get a real feel for what people have to live. We've all heard what you did as a youth, but because it wasn't for you doesn't mean that we should incarcerate all of them. Please have an open mind, that will get you so much further than the normal political bull that most politicians spew. I think a lot of people are tired of the lies and the hiding. If you feel something is the right thing or the wrong thing say it and don't be afraid, be honest with the people. They will respect you for your candor. I honestly feel that is why you won the office, you didn't try to deny your past, you were honest with people about what you felt.

Once you show people that your idea will work, they will have no choice but to believe it, it won't take a lot to get there. As more and more young voters begin to turn out and use the internet and learn from real scientific data, you will see that the support will grow. You've got 4 years to bring this nation back to greatness and another 4 if you can prove to America that your policies will work to save our future.

-- Heathmo

Establish a Do Not Mail registry to prohibit junk mail, **37240 points**

Just like we have a Do Not Call registry, there should be a Do Not Mail registry. Companies that fail to comply with this registry should be hit with hefty fines and, if needed, criminal prosecution.

This registry should include ALL unwanted forms of mail, such as credit card offers, election materials, grocery store flyers...anything that we don't want to receive, we shouldn't be forced to.
-- *Joshua Coker*

END PAY-TO-PLAY CULTURE IN WASHINGTON, **28930 points**

The pay-to-play culture in Washington is the foremost reason that the public business is ignored by Congress in favor of a small number of well-funded special interest groups.

In fact, anyone who has worked in Washington knows that entire pieces of legislation are often written by these special interest groups and handed to the legislator to enact as-is. The implied deal is "you enact our legislation and we will continue to fund your election to office"; or conversely, "If you don't enact our legislation, we will stop funding your election to office and fund an opponent of yours that will enact our legislation."

THIS HAS TO STOP NOW!

My suggestion is to enact REAL campaign finance reform, in which all federal elections are funded by taxpayer dollars, and "reasonable" restrictions on the fee speech of so-called "independent" groups (527s) are put in place that ban campaign ads by these groups that occur within 90 days of a primary or general election.

This is the only way to stop these "scratch your head" votes in Congress, in which the public favors one course of action, but Congress enacts just the opposite of what the public demands (e.g., Iraq). Real change must start from this issue in Obama's first term, because without this reform, all the change legislation we want Obama to enact will be thwarted by special interests in Washington that have their own agenda.
-- *Metteyya*

Enact more laws that protect the welfare of American citizens and less laws that benefit Big Banks and Big Corporations, **27490 points**

The power needs to be given back to the people. We need more protections from fraudulent, irresponsible, and unethical behavior of big corporations. We should not allow big business to take advantage of us and write our laws that benefit them and not the people. Let's turn our Corporatocracy back into a Democracy, of the people, by the people and for the people.
-- *JimBO*

Marriage Equality, **26400 points**

Across the country, same-sex couples do not have equal rights under the law; they are denied many of the benefits and protections that our local, state and federal governments provide to opposite-sex married couples. Why?

Instead, let us provide the same legal benefits and security to all families in America, whether they be formed by heterosexual couples or homosexual couples. Let us have marriage equality. Let's not hold on to this form of legal discrimination for decades after other democratic nations have let it go.

I was sad to see a constitutional amendment passed last year in my home state of California which banned gay marriage, shortly following a decision by the state's supreme court declaring that the state constitution protects a fundamental "right to marry" that extends equally to same-sex couples. Why would we turn around again and deny that fundamental right to so many people?

To those who demand that we define "marriage" as a union of one man and one woman, I say: when this notion is instituted into our laws, it is discriminatory, and not in line with the principles of the U.S. Constitution. If you insist on defining marriage in this way, then marriage is something that belongs strictly in our churches; then we must remove "marriage" from our laws, tax codes, etc., and instead have "civil union" or "domestic partnership" laws which provide the same legal protections and benefits to everyone.

-- kevhav

Credit, **25970 points**

Credit scores and checks should be used for only credit offers. One's credit should not be taken into account when applying for a job, applying for insurance or any thing not directly related to a loan since that is what credit really is.

This actually puts a stranglehold on people who have a hiccup in their credit early in their careers as credit can vanish instantly but can take years to recover from even playing and paying by the rules. One period of a few months can negatively affect a persons life by not allowing for promotion, increased insurance payments, unable to apply for another job and have to stick to menial labor.

-- Justin

Provide dis-incentives for suburban sprawl, **24170 points**

Every city has countless pockets of real estate activity: a seperate area for residential space, another for commercial. You drive past miles and miles of stores before you see anywhere to live. Or past subdivision after subdivision before you see any retail. And far too many cities have 4, 6, or 8 lane highways with no way for pedestrians or people on bikes to cross without treat of death.

It's time to charge higher taxes for any developments that don't include mixed use spaces: let's stop encouraging developers to build spaces that are only good for one thing, and require us to drive miles for anything else. There are countless cities in Europe where people don't even need a car, because they can walk or take a train or bus. Americans deserve the same.

-- Joshua Coker

Bush Administration Investigation, **23820 points**

I can well understand President Obama desiring to look ahead and leave the Bush Era behind, yet am well aware of President Ford's pardon of Nixon which ended his political career and forever cast a cloud over his Presidency. Because many Americans feel very badly about the Bush years, I suggest perhaps a review of the political and social ramifications of simply allowing history to take its course. The potential war crimes will have lasting affects upon foreign policy for decades and the economic meltdown screams of malfeasance by the entire administration. While I am not politically qualified as is President Obama, I fear failing to at least appoint an independent panel or office to research could prove disasterous to the new administration. Forgive my intrusion into politics.

-- Fish

No Raise for Congress, **23400 points**

I propose Congress not get thier (annual) pay raise of $4700.00 this year. They should not get one more cent of our tax dollars until the budget is balanced, the recession is over and Americans trust thier judgement.

-- tdiddle